TOUCH WOOD

A resource exploring
the words of Jesus
on the cross

PETE TOWNSEND

First published in 2000 by
KEVIN MAYHEW LTD
Buxhall
Stowmarket
Suffolk IP14 3BW

© 2000 Pete Townsend

The right of Pete Townsend to be identified as the author
of this work has been asserted by him in accordance
with the Copyright, Designs and Patents Act, 1988.

The drama sketches may be photocopied without
copyright infringement, provided they are used for the
purpose for which they are intended.
Reproduction of any of the contents of this
book for commercial purposes is subject to the
usual copyright restrictions.

No other part of this publication may be reproduced,
stored in a retrieval system, or transmitted, in any form
or by any means, electronic, mechanical, photocopying,
recording or otherwise, without the prior written
permission of the publisher.

All rights reserved.

Scripture quotations are from the *Contemporary English Version* © American Bible Society 1991, 1992, 1995. Used by permission. Anglicisations © British and Foreign Bible Society 1997.

0 1 2 3 4 5 6 7 8 9

ISBN 1 84003 664 8
Catalogue No. 1500402

Cover design by Jonathan Stroulger
Illustrated by David Bill
Edited and typeset by Elisabeth Bates
Printed and bound in Great Britain

Contents

Acknowledgements	4
Introduction	5
How to use this book	7
Father, forgive them	9
You shall be with me	17
Woman, behold your son	27
Why have you rejected me?	33
I thirst	43
It is finished	51
Father, I give you my life	59

Acknowledgements

Touch Wood was originally performed by a group of friends one cold and grey Saturday night. So, many thanks to Chris, Ian, Anne and Geoff for bringing life to the words and depth to the characters. Thanks also to Colin, Dave, Robin, Steph, George and Judith for adding a musical note. And to Dave and John for shedding a little light on the subject. Cheers, Paul, for helping shift all the gear. Thanks to Billy for his amazing artwork.

Most of all, love and hugs to Ruth for sharing a life.

Introduction

Touch Wood takes a close look at a few short hours in the life and death of Jesus Christ. All the other 289,080 hours of his life find their fulfilment in the last moments that Jesus drew breath.

Although Jesus had mentioned the manner of his death many times before, everybody failed to understand what he meant or chose not to believe that something so horrific could happen. After years of oppression by the Romans with their foreign culture, traditions and religious practices and the overbearing reign of a succession of violent kings, the kingdom of Israel was in desperate need of a Saviour, the Messiah.

Under Roman occupation the average person would have had to pay three types of tax: a poll tax, paid by everyone within the Roman Empire apart from Roman citizens; a land tax which was payable by anyone who owned land, and a tax on goods and sales. Added to this, the Jews were expected to pay a tax to maintain the temple and a percentage of their income to keep the priests in food and clothes. No wonder that there were many groups who dreamed of being set free from physical and economic domination!

At first many thought that John the Baptist was going to be the one to bring salvation to Israel, but he spoke of someone to come whose sandals John wasn't good enough even to carry! Anticipation ran high.

And, at last, here was someone with just the right touch. His words were revolutionary, his actions upset some people and healed others. His very presence attracted large crowds and the word 'Messiah' was being whispered on street corners. Expectations as well as anticipation were high.

Crowds lined the streets as Jesus entered Jerusalem on a donkey. This wasn't quite what the people expected. Tradition stated that when a king went to war it was on a horse. Riding a donkey signified a king coming in peace. But peace isn't what followed.

First the stallholders in the temple were sorted out, then Jesus has some harsh words for the teachers of the Law of Moses and then he goes on to talk about the temple being destroyed! Before long a plot to kill Jesus was being put into action.

After a last supper with his disciples, Jesus is arrested and asked whether he considers himself to be the Messiah. Jesus' reply of 'If you say so!' is enough to sentence him to death. The Chief Priests are really chuffed that at last they've got Jesus where they want him. But, there was still one snag. Pilate always released one prisoner during the time of the Passover. With a bit of encouragement from the Priests, the same crowd that had welcomed Jesus into Jerusalem now called for his death and the release of the prisoner Barabbas. You can imagine the relief on the face of Barabbas: 'Phew, that was close. At least I won't have to face the death penalty again, touch wood.' Jesus had no reason to place his trust in superstition. His intention was to touch wood for an entirely different reason.

The journey of Jesus with the cross and the account of his last breath are detailed in each of the sections which deal with one of the particular 'sayings of the cross' as found in the Gospels. Each saying reveals a characteristic of Jesus' life and his determination to make a relationship with God the Father possible for everyone for all time. Jesus didn't keep his fingers crossed hoping that everything would go as planned. He had no charm bracelet or lucky pair of sandals. He had no superstitious belief about black cats or throwing salt cellars over his shoulder at the last supper. Jesus held firmly to the belief that he was doing exactly what his Father wanted and that his ultimate sacrifice was the only way to tear down the barrier between God and the world. There was no other way. Jesus gritted his teeth, put his back into it and *touched wood*.

How to use this book

Touch Wood can be used as an encouragement for personal devotion or as a resource for collective worship. Each of the sections is self-contained and provides a complete resource for use either as a one-off session or as part of a series of integrated studies that explore each of the sayings of the cross.

Each section is divided into eight parts:

Bible passage
A Gospel reading containing one of the sayings of the cross.

Sketch
A drama sketch that can be used to explore the Bible passage from a different perspective.

Song
A suggestion for a worship song which reflects the theme.

Summary
Some thoughts and insights which expand the theme further.

Questions
Three questions which encourage the reader to think and meditate on the theme.

Background

An insight into the culture, traditions or facts that help the reader appreciate the background to the Bible passage.

Song

A second suggestion for worship.

Prayer

Two prayers which explore the theme and its relevance. The first prayer, 'Inner', concentrates on the individual, while the second prayer, 'Outer', looks at the theme from a group point of view.

The drama sketch can be kept fairly simple using the minimum numbers of actors and props or performed using the suggestions within the script and any other ideas you may have.

The worship songs are taken from *The source new songs 1* and *Re:source 2000* (Kevin Mayhew, 1999) and are only suggestions which can be altered to suit.

Touch Wood is intended to provoke a reaction, even if it causes you to question, complain and generally get irritated, take it up with God the Father. I think God would rather enjoy having a chat with you; after all, isn't that why Jesus put his back against the wood of the cross in the first place?

Father, forgive them

As Jesus was being led away, some soldiers grabbed hold of a man from Cyrene named Simon. He was coming in from the fields, but they put the cross on him and made him carry it behind Jesus.

A large crowd was following Jesus, and in the crowd a lot of women were crying and weeping for him. Jesus turned to the women and said: 'Women of Jerusalem, don't cry for me! Cry for yourselves and for your children. Some day people will say, "Women who never had children are really fortunate!" At that time everyone will say to the mountains, "Fall on us!" They will say to the hills, "Hide us!" If this happens when the wood is green, what do you think will happen when it is dry?'

Two criminals were led out to be put to death with Jesus. When the soldiers came to the place called 'The Skull', they nailed Jesus to a cross. They also nailed the two criminals to crosses, one on each side of Jesus.

Jesus said, 'Father, forgive these people! They don't know what they are doing.' While the crowd stood there watching Jesus, the soldiers gambled for his clothes. The leaders insulted him by saying, 'He saved others. Now he should save himself, if he really is God's chosen Messiah!'

Luke 23:26-35

The prisoners

The scene is a prison cell somewhere east of Skegness. Two prisoners are passing the time away (before it passes away completely) with a bit of chat and the occasional smile. The prisoners are feeling less than happy about their predicament but are puzzled by another prisoner who left a few moments ago. Why was he so calm? Why wasn't he terrified at the prospect of being tortured and strapped to a cross? Wasn't he worried about getting splinters? Before they have time to chat any further, a guard comes along to take them on a little walk through the town and up a hill, where they will be given a lift up so that they can admire the view. You never know, they might meet up with that guy they met earlier.

Characters   Two petty crooks whose expertise and cunning are only rivalled by a bag of jelly babies.

Scene   Inside a prison cell. Shadows of bars fall across the two prisoners' faces. Sitting nervously, they cast glances about them. Not sure what will happen next they both sit hunched-up.

Props   Two benches or small seats. Chains around the hands and legs of the crooks. A projector or spotlight to project the shadows of bars.

Convict (*Looks around nervously. Looks sideways at Villain*) What are you in here for?

Villain (*Doesn't look at Convict*) It's a bit embarrassing really.

Convict You don't look like a bloke who can get embarrassed easily. Not with a haircut like that.

Villain (*Looks at Convict*) You can talk. Looks like you got dressed with whatever you found on the washing line.

Convict (*Sniffs*) I did.

Villain Must have been in a bit of a hurry, then.

Convict I was, mate. Matter of life and death.

Villain (*Folds arms across chest*) Well it certainly is now.

Convict What?

Villain Life and death. I hope you enjoyed what you had because there doesn't seem much hope of extending your life insurance policy.

Convict Insurance salesmen! Bunch of robbers. It's them who should be in here, not law-abiding citizens like me and you.

Villain Not quite law-abiding. Perhaps a citizen who's got a different interpretation of the law to some. A kind of flexible approach. I like to bend it my way.

Both characters remain quiet for a few moments. In the background can be heard the sounds of shouting, a cell door is slammed shut and chains rattle.

Convict (*Shakes head slowly from side to side*) So anyway, what are you in here for?

Villain Joyriding.

Convict Joyriding! Is that all? How on earth did you get caught?

Villain Couldn't get the donkey to wake up.

Convict	And some early morning guard nabbed you then?
Villain	No. I went to fetch some carrots from the local store.
Convict	And then you got nabbed? Isn't that breaking and entering?
Villain	No, well yes, technically. You see, I suddenly remembered I hadn't had any breakfast, so I munched my way through the fruit section and then moved on to the deli counter.
Convict	And then what?
Villain	I fell asleep.
Convict	And then you felt the long arm of the law prod you into consciousness?
Villain	No, it was the storekeeper's wife with her broom.
Convict	*(Winces)* Ooh, that could have been nasty. So, how come you got done for joyriding?
Villain	I tried to make my getaway on the donkey. *(Faint sound of hooves 'clip-clop' on stone road)* I had to escape.
Convict	So would I, mate, with a broom about to interfere with my anatomy. Anyway, that's still not joyriding, merely trying to escape from a severe bout of broomitis.
Villain	It's called joyriding when the donkey races off like lightning with me hanging on to its tail. Up-ended six priests, two tax collectors and a soothsayer before they caught me. So, what's your story?
Convict	I'm in for domestic violence.
Villain	Can't you sort out your domestic squabbles in private?
Convict	Wish I could. They put me in here for my own protection. You haven't seen the wife. Muscles the size of temple pillars. Makes me shudder to think. *(Looks nervously around)*
Villain	Still, a bit steep putting you in here over a tiff.

Convict	That's what I tried to tell them. But some bright spark recognised me from a wanted poster.
Villain	What you wanted for then, throwing a tantrum in the bath?
Convict	I was spotted trying to rob the local tax collector's office.
Villain	You should have used a look-out.
Convict	I did. I was told he was the best in the business.
Villain	Who's that, then?
Convict	Blind Bartimaeus.
Villain	But he *is* blind!
Convict	I just thought it was his nickname. You know, sort of turns a blind eye to things.
Villain	He definitely did that.
Convict	Bit of bad luck that, really.
Villain	Yeah. Still, not so unlucky as the bloke who was in here earlier.
Convict	Who was that, then?
Villain	Some religious teacher who got caught up in a bit of politics.
Convict	Politics. It'll be the death of us.
Villain	It will, mate, take my word for it. But this bloke, he sounded an OK sort of guy. I heard he was some sort of teacher. Upset a few of the local big noises but his heart was in the right place.
Convict	Bet he was really narked at being thrown in here and then put on trial.
Villain	Now, that's the funny thing. He didn't seem to mind, sort of expected it. Didn't hold a grudge.
Convict	I heard he did a lot of amazing things. Someone told me he even healed Blind Bartimaeus.

Villain	He'll have to get another nickname now.
Convict	He might make a better look-out though.
Villain	Yeah, at least things are looking up for him.
Convict	I think things will be looking up for us soon. *(Looks in the direction of the light projecting image of prison bars)*
Villain	Yeah, looking up at a great chunk of wood waiting for our attention.
Convict	Oh well, beats work.

Sound of another cell door being slammed and loud footsteps echo along the corridor. A key is heard turning in the lock and a cell door creaks open.

Villain	Talking of beating, here comes that guard with the welcoming snarl.

'On the blood-stained ground' by Graham Kendrick (*The source new songs,* 47).

At his trial, Jesus must have felt that the whole world was against him. There were those who openly opposed him and had done everything they could to silence a voice that threatened to disrupt their egocentric lifestyles. There were those people who wanted to dispose of a voice that openly criticised their religious activity (an activity which said more about their devotion to themselves and rituals than their devotion to God). And there were those who wept. They wept because they felt a sense of loss, a sense of defeat and a sense of betrayal. They felt betrayed by those followers of Jesus who faded into the background when things began to get tough. The felt betrayed by their own emotions which had hoped for so much and now saw all their desires crumble under a whip. But the one who was betrayed and had suffered the biting lashes of rejection wouldn't have chosen any other way. This was the way forward, the way chosen by his Father.

TOUCH WOOD

1. Wouldn't Jesus have had a greater and longer-lasting impact on the world if he'd proved to everyone that he was God's Son by performing a miracle and 'saving' himself?

   He suffered and endured great pain for us, but we thought his suffering was punishment from God. He was wounded and crushed because of our sins; by taking our punishment, he made us completely well. All of us were like sheep that had wandered off. We each had gone our own way, but the Lord gave him the punishment we deserved. He was painfully abused, but he did not complain. He was silent like a lamb being led to the butcher, as quiet as a sheep having its wool cut off. He was condemned to death without a fair trial. Who could have imagined what would happen to him? His life was taken away because of the sinful things my people had done. He wasn't dishonest or violent, but he was buried in a tomb of cruel and rich people. The Lord decided his servant would suffer as a sacrifice to take away the sin and guilt of others. Now the servant will live to see his own descendants. He did everything the Lord had planned. By suffering, the servant will learn the true meaning of obeying the Lord. Although he is innocent, he will take the punishment for the sins of others, so that many of them will no longer be guilty. The Lord will reward him with honour and power for sacrificing his life. Others thought he was a sinner, but he suffered for our sins and asked God to forgive us.   Isaiah 53:4-12

2. How do we react when everything seems to be against us?

3. When something happens in a way we don't expect, does it mean we may have got things wrong?

The crucifixion was a barbaric form of punishment. The suffering and obvious pain were all part of a process designed to act as a warning to anyone who had thoughts of rebellion against the system.

When the person to be crucified reached the place of crucifixion, the T-shaped cross (there was no extended top piece so that the person had nowhere to rest their head) was placed upon the ground and the person's arms were stretched out across the bar and their hands nailed to the wood. The feet were fastened to the upright. About half-way up the cross was a piece of wood called the 'saddle'. This was designed to take the weight of the victim so they didn't tear their hands from the nails. The 'cross' was then lifted into a socket which kept the person's feet about a metre above the ground.

Dragging the heavy wooden cross through the streets (often going the long way round) and the subsequent nails and lifting into position were excruciatingly painful but not designed to kill the victim immediately. The victim was left to die of a mixture of pain, thirst and starvation.

'For the cross' by Matt Redman (*Re:source 2000*, 6).

Inner (Place a wooden cross in the centre of the room. Read the prayer facing the cross.)

Lord,
    I cannot begin to understand the pain,
    thirst, hunger or humiliation.
It's totally beyond my comprehension.
It's totally beyond my imagination.
It's totally beyond me
    why you would go through so much
    for me.
You meant so much to everyone
    who had followed your every move,
    listened to your every word
    and watched, amazed at your every action.
You had the chance to turn around,
    walk away
    and live to share your heart
    another day.
But you chose to face the cross,
    to put yourself
    in the hands
    of everyone
    who wanted you silenced,
    inactive,
    out of sight,
    extinct, totally dead.
They thought they'd won
    but we know better,
    or at least
    we should do.

Outer
(Stand in front of the cross and stretch your arms out in front of you with the palms of your hands facing upwards.)

Lord,
    you suffered,
    knew rejection,
    endured insults,
    were falsely accused
    and paid the price.
All around,
    wherever the winds blow,
    there are people
    suffering,
    imprisoned,
    rejected by those who know them,
    falsely accused;
    and waiting
    for someone
    to speak their name,
    free them of the chains
    that shackle them
    to the walls of persecution.
Hear their cry, Lord,
    bring comfort,
    dry their tears,
    fill their hearts
    with the warmth
    of your love.
Teach us,
    show us
    how we,
    each one of us,
    can reach out
    and be the voice
    of the voiceless.
To stand for those
    who cannot stand.
Be their light
    wherever darkness falls.
Amen.

You shall be with me

The soldiers made fun of Jesus and brought him some wine. They said, 'If you are the king of the Jews, save yourself!' Above him was a sign that said, 'This is the King of the Jews'.

One of the criminals hanging there also insulted Jesus by saying, 'Aren't you the Messiah? Save yourself and save us!'

But the other criminal told the first one off: 'Don't you fear God? Aren't you getting the same punishment as this man? We got what was coming to us, but he didn't do anything wrong.' Then he said to Jesus, 'Remember me when you come into power!'

Jesus replied, 'I promise that today you will be with me in paradise.'

Luke 23:36–43

The hitchhikers

On a rough track north of somewhere, a man stands waiting. He's not alone although he would like to be. A fresh-faced hiker, complete with brand-new rucksack and clean shoes, joins him. A discussion soon develops about life on the road and where it's all leading to. Neither of the hikers knows where they're going, or where they've been for that matter. They have no idea what may be waiting for them if they ever get anywhere. One hiker would rather wait and let nothing happen while the other is willing to throw caution to the wind and put one foot in front of the other and hurtle forward into the unknown. Neither of them has the security of knowing what lies ahead or if anyone will be waiting for them if they ever arrive. Does anybody care?

Characters	Two hitchhikers: one who has seen better days and the other who hopes to see better days. The first hitchhiker has a weather-beaten, 'seen-it-all-before' attitude while the other hitchhiker is full of energy and enthusiasm.
Scene	A darkened, lonely road. One world-weary hitchhiker is nonchalantly ignoring the world while a second hitchhiker approaches him.
Props	Hitchhiker 1 has a tatty coat, grubby wellingtons and a holey rucksack. He's holding a card which reads: 'Gonroamin'. Hitchhiker 2 has a bright coloured waterproof coat, walking boots and a new rucksack. He holds a card which reads: 'Newhere'.
Hitch 1	*(Initially ignores the second hitchhiker but, after a few seconds, stops looking at the stars and slowly turns to face the newcomer)* You'll have a long wait if you think there's any chance of getting a lift tonight.

Hitch 2	That bad, is it?
Hitch 1	Bad? *(Sniffs)* I was in nursery school when I first came here.
Hitch 2	Nobody ever going your way, then?
Hitch 1	*(Shrugs shoulders)* I'm really not bothered which way I go as long as I'm not here. *(Rubs sleeve across 'Gonroamin' card)*
Hitch 2	Doesn't it depend on which side of the road you're standing?
Hitch 1	Does it matter? *(Tilts head to resume study of the night sky)*
Hitch 2	It does if you want to go north and you're standing on the south-bound side of the road.
Hitch 1	*(Remains looking skywards)* It doesn't matter which way I go. I feel as if I've been stuck on life's central reservation.
Hitch 2	*(Shrugs shoulders. Leans forward and looks into distance)* Hang on. I think there's something coming. *(Holds out 'Newhere' card)*
Hitch 1	*(Keeps looking skywards)* Don't get too excited. People are pretty suspicious of hitchhikers. Think we're some sort of alien species looking for someone to tow our flying saucer.

Sound of car in the distance.

Hitch 2	*(Begins to 'thumb' a lift and wave card)* We might be in luck. They're slowing down.
Hitch 1	*(Looks at other hitchhiker and tuts. Drops his card on the floor)* That's another thing. They think they're in the genius league because they think they've conned you into thinking you're going to get a lift. As soon as they get near you they race off laughing. IQ to match their shoe size.

Sound of car disappearing into the distance.

Hitch 2	*(Waves fist at disappearing car)* An intellect only rivalled by garden tools?
Hitch 1	Something like that.

Hitchhiker 1 resumes his search of the stars while the second hitchhiker hums tunelessly and continues his search for a potential lift by looking up and down the road.

Hitch 2	*(Sighs with exasperation)* Don't you get fed up waiting for a lift?
Hitch 1	*(Shrugs)* Not really. You do get to meet some interesting people all wanting to know where I'm going.
Hitch 2	Do you tell them?
Hitch 1	I would if I knew myself.
Hitch 2	What about your card then?
Hitch 1	*(Picks card up)* It's a statement not a place.
Hitch 2	So what do you tell all those people who ask?
Hitch 1	Depends what mood I'm in. Sometimes I tell them I'm a piece of living sculpture and I put my hand out for a contribution towards my living expenses. Other times I tell them to mind their own business.
Hitch 2	What do they say to that?
Hitch 1	They sometimes tell me where to go!
Hitch 2	*(Grins)* Bet that's helpful, especially if you haven't made your own mind up yet. *(Looks up and down the road again)* Doesn't their advice get on your nerves?
Hitch 1	Not as much as people expecting *me* to know where I want to go.
Hitch 2	Bit difficult wanting to go somewhere without directions.
Hitch 1	*(Begins to sound irritated)* Look, if I wanted directions I would have consulted a map, not a talking parrot.
Hitch 2	No need to get shirty. Just making conversation. I doubt if you hear much news on your journey nowhere.
Hitch 1	News hasn't got any interest for me. What's the point of having news about somewhere you'd rather not be or about a place you're not going to?

Hitch 2 Point taken. But surely you'd like to keep up with gossip?

Hitch 1 You can't leave it alone can you?

Hitch 2 Only trying to help.

Sound of thunderstorm and rain

Hitch 1 *(Hunches shoulders and turns up the collar of his coat against the rain)* Well, help yourself to a patch of grass somewhere else and leave me behind.

Hitch 2 What are you leaving behind then?

Hitch 1 Not a lot.

Hitch 2 Family, friends?

Hitch 1 Would be if I had any.

Hitch 2 Surely someone will miss you?

Hitch 1 Not really. I made sure no one would be looking for me.

Hitch 2 How's that?

Hitch 1 Left all my clothes and sandals in a neat pile in one of those toilet cubicles at a motorway service station.

Hitch 2 Why?

Hitch 1 Why not?

Hitch 2 You might have made the cleaning staff a lot of extra work.

Hitch 1 How do you make that out?

Hitch 2 They would have spent ages searching each of the cubicles for you and then had to call a plumber out.

Hitch 1 That's their business.

Hitch 2 You can say that again. Anyway, why all the secrecy?

Hitch 1	I don't want anyone to know where I'm going.
Hitch 2	But you don't even know that yourself!
Hitch 1	See, it worked!
Hitch 2	Let me get this straight. You don't want to be followed.
Hitch 1	Yeah.
Hitch 2	So, to make sure no one follows you, you don't know where you're going.
Hitch 1	That's right.
Hitch 2	So, what's the point?
Hitch 1	There isn't one. If I had a point I'd be heading somewhere.
Hitch 2	I don't think I could live like that.
Hitch 1	That's a good job. If it did make sense you'd be following me and that's precisely what I don't want.
Hitch 2	Well, I can't stay here, I've got to move on.
Hitch 1	Give my regards to wherever you're going.
Hitch 2	I will if I ever get there.

Hitch 1 resumes his search of the stars as Hitch 2 adjusts his rucksack and ambles off.

'How do I know you love me?' by Mark Altrogge (*The source new songs*, 19).

The crucifixion of Jesus with two criminals was not a mere coincidence. By positioning Jesus between the two criminals the authorities were attempting to make a statement. First, that Jesus was no more than a common criminal, a thief or con artist. Second, a crown of thorns and a placard declaring him to be a king was intended to imply that he was nothing more than a leader of other criminals, a self-professed lord and liar.

Jesus is mocked by three groups of people. The leaders, or Jewish rulers, mock him with a sense of relief. To them, Jesus posed a threat, a constant thorn in their side who reminded them of their duty to God and to the community. It came as a huge sense of relief to the authorities when Jesus was 'put in his place' and humiliated. It was a public statement that implied Jesus had been judged by the real leaders and found to be a fraud whose followers were nothing more than a bunch of no-hopers.

The soldiers had mocked Jesus by again questioning his ability to do anything about his situation. To the soldiers, a leader was someone to be respected, someone who held authority and whose orders were obeyed. They despised someone who claimed to have authority but who received nothing more than public disgrace.

The two criminals who were crucified with Jesus mocked him because it appeared that he'd been brought down to their level. To be crucified with them meant he was no better than them and was someone who wasn't clever enough, or powerful enough, to avoid the punishment of a common criminal.

Almost immediately the criminals realised that an innocent person was being crucified. One of the criminals understood that Jesus was taking the blame for the crimes of other people.

A little while later a Roman officer began to praise God after recognising that Jesus was everything he claimed to be. And it wasn't long before the authorities realised that their attempt to kill Jesus was nothing more than a fulfilment of everything Jesus had said would happen. Their mockery died as Jesus rose from the dead.

1. Why was Jesus considered to be such a threat to the religious authorities?

For a short time the religious authorities welcomed the words that initially John the Baptist and then Jesus used to encourage people to a faith in God. But, it wasn't long before they realised that Jesus considered them, the religious leaders, to be as far from a real relationship with God as anyone else. Even more worrying was the fact that Jesus didn't encourage the people to go through the religious procedures and customs considered so important by the religious leaders. In fact, Jesus pointed out the hypocrisy of the religious leaders who abused their positions of power for their own selfish reasons. Little wonder that the religious leaders thought they'd be better off with Jesus dead.

YOU SHALL BE WITH ME

> *Then some Pharisees and teachers of the law came to Jesus from Jerusalem. They asked him, 'Why don't your followers obey the unwritten laws which have been handed down to us? They don't wash their hands before they eat.' Jesus answered, 'And why do you refuse to obey God's command so that you can follow your own teachings? . . . You are hypocrites! Isaiah was right when he said about you: "These people show honour to me with words, but their hearts are far from me. Their worship is worthless. The things they teach are nothing but human rules."'*
>
> *And Jesus called the crowd to him, and said, 'Listen and understand what I am saying. It is not what people put into their mouths that makes them unclean. It is what comes out of their mouths that makes them unclean.'*
>
> Matthew 15:1-3, 7-11

2. What would have been your thoughts if you'd been a follower of Jesus and now you stood watching him being crucified?

3. What do you think made the criminals change their minds about Jesus?

Jesus told one of the criminals: '. . . I promise that today you will be with me in paradise' (Luke 23:43). The word 'Paradise' is of Persian origin meaning 'a walled garden'. It was custom for a Persian king to grant one of his subjects a special honour by asking him to join the king for a walk in the royal gardens.

'Should he who made the stars' by Mark Altrogge (*The source new songs*, 57).

Inner
(Have a large cross positioned in the centre of the room. At the base of the cross is an empty cardboard box. You will need a selection of personal items which will be placed in the box during the prayer. Begin by standing next to the cross.)

23

TOUCH WOOD

Lord,
    here I am
    just as you asked.
So, what can I do for you?
Excuse me?
To give?
Really, is that all?
Well, that's soon sorted. (*Fumble in pocket for some coins and then place them in the box*)
Right, how's that?
Pardon?
Not quite what you expected.
Well, I'm sorry but it's been a bad month,
    what with the telephone bill, TV licence,
    gas bill, magazine subscriptions, haircut,
    and there were those special offers at the supermarket –
    you know, buy one get one free.
That's a thought,
    would you like a bottle of disinfectant? (*Put bottle in the box*)
It's all right, I've got another twenty-three at home.
Still not what you expected?
(*Take wallet out of pocket*)
Here, there's my credit card –
    although it won't do you a lot of good,
    it's almost up to its limit. (*Throw card into box*)
Here's my library card,
    video store card –
    they're half-price if you return them before 5pm.
Still not interested?
Hmm, what about my shoes. (*Place in box*)
You might have a use for the disinfectant now.
Here's my shirt, (*Place in box*)
    my watch (*place in box*)
    and my jacket I had last Christmas. (*Place in box*)
Excuse me?
You're still not interested?
Hey, there's no pleasing some people
    is there?
What?
You still want me to give?
But you've got virtually everything,
    except my CD collection,
But hey, come on,

there are limits you know.
Pardon?
No limits?
To giving.
Oh, I suppose you're right
    there is something else *(Stand in box)*
    there's always me.

Outer

(Kneel in front of the cross.)

Lord,
    you gave everything,
    you risked the lot
    so that
    I, we, all, every breathing person
    could know
    what it's like
    to live
    without the weight of guilt
    sitting on our shoulders
    reminding us
    every second of the day
    that there was never
    going to be a way
    to experience life
    the way you intended it to be
    with
    me, we, all, every breathing person
    being able
    to know you
    as our Father.
My words
    could never express
    what it feels like
    to be wanted so much
    and to be loved
    by you
    because you care
    for me, we, all, every breathing person.

Woman, behold your son

Then Pilate handed Jesus over to be nailed to a cross. Jesus was taken away, and he carried his cross to a place known as 'The Skull'. In Aramaic this place is called 'Golgotha'. There Jesus was nailed to the cross, and on each side of him a man was also nailed to a cross. Pilate ordered the charge against Jesus to be written on a board and put above the cross. It read, 'Jesus of Nazareth, King of the Jews'. The words were written in Hebrew, Latin and Greek. The place where Jesus was taken wasn't far from the city, and many of the Jewish people read the charge against him. So the chief priests went to Pilate and said, 'Why did you write that he is King of the Jews? You should have written, "He claimed to be King of the Jews."' But Pilate told them, 'What is written will not be changed!' After the soldiers had nailed Jesus to the cross, they divided up his clothes into four parts, one for each of them. But his outer garment was made from a single piece of cloth, and it did not have any seams. The soldiers said to each other, 'Let's not rip it apart. We will gamble to see who gets it.' This happened so that the Scriptures would come true, which say,

   'They divided up my clothes and gambled for my garments.'
The soldiers then did what they decided.

   Jesus' mother stood beside his cross with her sister and Mary the wife of Clopas. Mary Magdalene was standing there too. When Jesus saw his mother and his favourite disciple with her, he said to his mother, 'This man is now your son.' Then he said to the disciple, 'She is now your mother.' From then on, that disciple took her into his own home.   John 19:16-27

So close, Mary

Watching life fade is something that nobody wants to see. But looking up at a life that means so much to you is an experience you never want to happen. It's all happening so close yet so far away. The frustration of being close enough to see the sweat bead on his forehead yet too far away to wipe them away is agony. And now, the life that means so much doesn't think of his own suffering but wants to make sure that his mother will be cared for. While his body cries out to have his mother's arms around him, to comfort him, he ensures that she has arms to comfort her.

Character   Mary, Jesus' mother is standing alone. She is feeling emotionally desolate.

Scene   Mary is standing apart from the crowd. She needs to be alone to grieve as only a mother can. The lighting is sombre, casting dark shadows. Her clothes are an expression of her heart: blue and lifeless.

> *Props* Spotlight with different coloured gels (blue, green, red), clothing dark, possibly blue, with head-scarf made of a reflective material.

This is to be performed as a monologue. The only interaction is between the actor and the lighting. The overall feeling is to be intimate, a heart expression of Mary.

Start with lighting dark. Single colour to highlight Mary (blue).

Mary stands slightly to one side and facing across the stage. She looks into the distance.

The last few days have been awful. It's impossible to describe the feeling in your stomach. As if something is tearing your insides, clawing at your heart, draining your life away. *(Slight pause)*

I always knew something like this would happen. I'd put it to the back of my mind, not wanting to think about it, not giving the thoughts space to develop, to take form in my head. *(Sigh)* It's easier to get through each day by dismissing them as leftovers from some nightmare, some ghost of a memory that is best left at the edge of consciousness. *(Take deep breath)*

But now reality has arrived like a thunderstorm on a summer's day. The nightmare has arrived. Those thoughts which had been buried in the deepest recesses of my mind, *(Hand held to side of head)* have now stormed into the light of day. *(Change lighting to brighter colour, e.g. yellow)*

(Look upwards, still with hand on side of the head) Looking at him is too painful. There is my son *(Hand moves from side of head and points vaguely in front of her)* whose birth was a miracle, whose life had taken form cocooned from the world within me, and now the world is taking him from me. His was the life which I had cradled in my arms *(Fold both arms across body). (Lighting colour: green)* His was the life which I saw grow each day. *(Arms move from body and open downwards as if welcoming a small child)*

His was the life which had fulfilled everything a mother could hope for. His is the life which is draining away before my eyes *(Hands move to cover eyes. Head is lowered). (Lighting colour: red)*

(Lift head and hold hands out in a questioning manner) Why have they done this to him? Was it so wrong to want the best for him? *(Pause)*

It's a mockery of life! I want to reach out to him *(Slight move forward with one hand)* and wipe his forehead, to wipe away the blood from his face, to hold him, hold him so tight. *(Hand moves across body in clutching motion)* Why? Why this? *(Move whole body to face audience)*

Why does everybody just watch? They know he shouldn't be suffering like this. If only I could reach out to him, to touch him. *(Pause)*

He looks so weak, so much pain. *(Gentle shake of the head)* He had so much to give and now they're taking everything! *(Lighting colour: blue)*

WOMAN, BEHOLD YOUR SON

(Angry voice) THAT'S MY SON YOU'RE KILLING! Let me hold him, let me feel his breath against my cheek, let me comfort him. *(Shoulders sag)*

This heat is unbearable. He's thirsty. *(Look around)* Someone, let him drink, please! Hasn't he endured enough? *(Turn head upwards)*

Oh heaven above, can't someone help him? Surely it wasn't supposed to be like this?

(Move head gradually from one side of the audience to the other) Look at all these faces, what are they waiting for? Didn't his life mean anything? Can you stand by and watch the last breath escape his lips without the least touch of guilt?

(Long pause. Thrust head forward) YOU'RE WATCHING MY CHILD DIE! *(Pause)*

How long can this go on? Whose heart will break first? It feels as if my own life is fading as I watch. My blood runs cold through my veins. I have no strength left, I can't go on. *(Sigh and turn to face distant side of stage)*

How can he go on? How can I watch my son go through such agony? *(Lighting colour: merge blue with red)*

Why does he deserve to die this way? He hasn't hurt anyone. He wasn't interested in their politics. Is this what life is all about? *(Hands held open in question)* Is this the politicians' answer? I don't care who's right and who's wrong. I care that my son's life is fading as each second passes. *(Pause. Head tilted towards the floor)* *(Lighting colour: blue)*

His life is precious to me. If no one else in the world loves him, I do! *(Head turns to face audience)* *(Lighting colour: red)* Why does this have to happen? *(Head bowed)*

'O, your hands of kindness' by Martin Smith (*The source new songs*, 54).

There is a legend which tells that Mary, the mother of Jesus, had woven a seamless outer garment as a gift for her son. It was the custom for a Jewish mother to give her son a special gift when he left home (see John 19:23).

Seeing the special garment being gambled over by the four Roman soldiers must have been especially difficult for Mary to deal with. Not only was her son dying in front of her eyes but his clothes meant nothing more to the soldiers than an excuse to play dice. Mary must have thought it particularly insensitive on the part of the soldiers to make it so obvious that her son's life was now worthless in the eyes of the law. But, Mary's gift held a special significance.

The garment is said to be a single, seamless piece of cloth. This is the exact description for the outer garments worn by the High Priest. The priest's main function was to act as the go-between or liaison between God and the people. The Latin for priest is *pontiflex*, which literally means *bridge-builder*, and the priest was acknowledged as the person to build the bridge between God and his people.

From the beginning of his ministry Jesus had worn the symbol of a *bridge-builder*. At the cross Jesus became the ultimate sacrifice and bridge-builder between God and the people. Although deeply distressing for Mary, the death of Jesus was essential for the relationship between ourselves and God to be restored.

1. Was all this suffering worth it?

   God loved the people of this world so much that he gave his only Son, so that everyone who has faith in him will have eternal life and never really die. God did not send his Son into the world to condemn its people. He sent him to save them! No one who has faith in God's Son will be condemned. But everyone who doesn't have faith in him has already been condemned for not having faith in God's only Son. John 3:16-18

2. Wasn't there some other way that Jesus could have become God's *bridge-builder*?

3. Was anyone to blame for Jesus' death?

An added agony for those being crucified was the flogging they received prior to being nailed onto the cross. Although already in pain as a result of dragging their cross through the streets and the nails being driven into their hands, the victim's back was an open wound laid against a piece of rough hewn wood ('. . . though my back is like a field that has just been ploughed' Psalm 129:3).

The flogging most often associated with crucifixion was known as *verberatio*. The leather whip would be made up of several thongs fitted with pieces of jagged lead and sharpened bone. The flogging would be carried out by a soldier who would flog the victim until either the soldier was exhausted or the officer told him to stop.

'Through the cross' by Mike Burn (*The source new songs*, 71).

Inner (Place a candle in the centre of the room. Sit or stand facing the candle as you read the prayer.)

Lord,
    here I am
    with eyes wide open,
    staring, gazing,
    just watching
    as time flickers by.
After a while
    things seem to blur,
    as the encroaching darkness
    bleeds into my reality.
It's all around me,
    prodding at my consciousness,
    nudging at my senses,
    threatening to overwhelm me.
It would be so easy
    to peer into the darkness,
    allow it to cover my eyes,
    cloud my being
    and envelop me
    in its clinging sightlessness.
I'm frightened, Lord.
The darkness
    hides the day.
It hangs over me
    like a storm cloud
    blotting out the sun.
Let the light of your love
    shine into my life,
    pushing away the shadows,
    turning night into day
    and tearing the fear
    from my eyes.
Let the warmth of your love
    hug me,
    embrace my being,
    turning the shivers of cold
    into a glow
    of reflected love.
Lord,
    be with me
    as I walk through each day.
Allow my life
    to reflect the sun.

Outer (Light a second candle and place it next to the first.)

Lord,
    where there is darkness
    let me bring
    the light of your life.
Where there is hatred
    let me bring
    your peace.
Where there is hurt
    let me bring
    comfort.
Where there is crying
    let me bring
    hope.
Lord,
    be with each of us,
    allow us
    to be your light
    in a world
    that often seems
    engulfed,
    cloaked
    in darkness.
Lord,
    wherever we are,
    help us to be
    your voice,
    your heart,
    your love.
Protect us
    as we try to bring
    light
    into the dark places.
Be with us
    each step of the way
    so that the shadows
    will disappear
    wherever your people
    call out your name.

Why have you rejected me?

When the soldiers had finished making fun of Jesus, they took off the robe. They put his own clothes back on him and led him off to be nailed to a cross. On the way they met a man from Cyrene named Simon, and they forced him to carry Jesus' cross. They came to a place named Golgotha, which means 'Place of a skull'. There they gave Jesus some wine mixed with a drug to ease the pain. But when Jesus tasted what it was, he refused to drink it. The soldiers nailed Jesus to a cross and gambled to see who would get his clothes. Then they sat down to guard him. Above his head they put a sign that told why he was nailed there. It read, 'This is Jesus, the King of the Jews'. The soldiers also nailed two criminals on crosses, one to the right of Jesus and the other to his left. People who passed by said terrible things about Jesus. They shook their heads and shouted, 'So you're the one who claimed you could tear down the temple and build it again in three days! If you are God's Son, save yourself and come down from the cross!' The chief priests, the leaders, and the teachers of the Law of Moses also made fun of Jesus. They said, 'He saved others, but he can't save himself. If he is the king of Israel, he should come down from the cross! Then we will believe him. He trusted God, so let God save him, if he wants to. He even said he was God's Son.' The two criminals also said cruel things to Jesus. At midday the sky turned dark and stayed that way until three o'clock. Then about that time Jesus shouted, 'Eli, Eli, lema sabachthani?' which means, 'My God, my God, why have you deserted me?'
                                                                Matthew 27:31-46

On the edge

Abandoned. Friendless. Cast-off. Disowned. Destitute. Renounced. Outcast. Forsaken. Deserted. Lonely. Isolated. Solitary. Relinquished. The words seem to go on and on, longer than life itself. But can any of these words express the feeling of total alienation, where it seems as if the whole universe has turned its back on its creator?

There are a myriad of things that make us feel isolated at times. Some situations can make you feel despair, as if there is no alternative but to give up, curl up in a dark corner, screw your eyes tight shut and hope the world goes away. The only problem is that when you eventually open your eyes everything appears to be the same as before!

Characters Two friends, Bob and Eric, are returning from a night on the town. Both are dressed in regulation football shirts and carry a bottle of beer.

	The third character, Blink, is wearing a simple white T-shirt and shorts. He's extremely nervous and is clutching a diving mask and snorkel.
Scene	Late at night and two friends are returning home after sampling a selection of liquid refreshment on offer at several watering holes! As they continue their journey over a bridge they notice someone standing on the parapet. Is it a bird? Is it a plane? Or is it someone testing their sense of balance? The two friends decide to go and investigate.
Props	Two football shirts for the friends, two bottles of beer, white T-shirt, pair of shorts, diving mask and snorkel. A series of chairs could be used to give the impression of a bridge parapet.

Use subdued lighting for the area of the 'bridge'. You could use a small lamp suspended from a beam to give the impression of a street light.

The sketch starts with the third person standing nervously on the 'bridge' as the two friends approach. They stop and stand under the lamp.

Eric (*Stands under the lamp and takes a swig from his bottle of beer*) Here we go, (*Takes another swig*) here we go, (*Takes another swig*) here we go.

Bob (*Takes a swig from his bottle of beer and then peers down the neck of the bottle*) It's all gone, (*Looks again down the neck of the bottle*) It's all gone, (*Shakes bottle*) It's all gone. (*Puts head on Eric's shoulder*)

Eric (*Pats Bob's head*) There, there, there, then. Don't get upset. All good things come to an end some time.

Bob (*Sobs on Eric's shoulder*)

Eric (*Pats Bob's head again*) Come on, pull yourself together. There's always another night. Come on, it must be well past your bedtime.

Bob (*Lifts head from Eric's shoulder*) I don't want to go to bed.

Eric It's the only way you'll get to see a new day.

Bob I don't have to go to sleep. Can't I just stay awake and wait for the new day to arrive?

Eric It wouldn't be a new day then. It'd just be today stretched a bit.

Bob I still don't want to go to bed.

Eric	Why not?
Bob	Because if I go to sleep then I'll wake up.
Eric	That's not so bad an ambition.
Bob	But when I wake up, it'll be tomorrow.
Eric	*(Takes a step back)* Your powers of deduction are staggering.
Bob	And tomorrow is Monday and you know what that means.

Bob and Eric look at each other.

Both	Work!

Bob and Eric put their heads on each other's shoulders and sob. Suddenly they hear someone call 'Hello'.

Blink	Hello? *(Fiddles with diving mask and snorkel nervously)*
Bob	*(Raises head and looks around)* Did you hear something?
Eric	*(Looks around)* Only you vibrating the wax in my ear.
Bob	Listen, I'm sure I heard something.
Blink	Hello.
Bob	There it is again.
Eric	*(Looks over towards the bridge)* It came from over there.
Bob	*(Calls towards the bridge)* Hello?
Blink	Hello, have you got the time?
Eric	I'm afraid I haven't. I couldn't catch it. It just flew straight past me.
Blink	*(Glumly)* Great, just what I need, another comedian. The world's full of people who think that life's a joke.
Bob	*(Nudges Eric)* He's had a few too many and got all depressed.
Blink	A few too many, eh? You're dead right. A few too many breakfasts. A

	few too many bank statements. A few too many gas bills. A few too many days wandering about on this planet.
Eric	*(Nudges Bob)* You're right. Certainly a few too many.
Bob	If you ask me he needs a few more.
Blink	I can't take any more of this *(Holds head with one hand while the other hand holds the diving mask and snorkel)*
Eric	*(Inclines head towards Blink)* Bit dramatic, eh?
Bob	Real drama merchant. Attention seeking I reckon.
Blink	*(Shakes head vigorously)* No, no, no. that's the last thing I want.
Eric	So, what are you doing standing up there, then?
Blink	*(Places diving mask on top of head)* You wouldn't understand.
Bob	He's right. I never could understand people who stand on bridges with a diving mask on their heads.
Blink	Go on, make fun. That's all I'm good for. An object of ridicule, a stimulus for laughter. *(Points snorkel at Bob)* You're just like all the rest.
Bob	If you mean like 'all the rest' who don't walk around with a diving mask on their heads, then yes, I suppose I am like all the rest.
Eric	Could prove useful though, the diving mask. Great idea for when you're peeling onions.
Bob	Or keeping the soap out of your eyes in the shower.
Eric	*(Nods towards Blink)* But he's not in the shower.
Bob	And he's definitely not peeling onions.
Eric	So what's he doing?
Bob	*(Turns to Blink)* Yeah, so what are you doing?
Blink	*(Stares in front of him)* Going to put an end to the laughter.

Bob	Easy, take the diving mask off.
Eric	I'd put the snorkel away as well if I were you.
Blink	*(Pulls diving mask over eyes)* Just be thankful you're not me.
Bob	*(Turns to Eric)* Eric?
Eric	Yeah?
Bob	Am I me?
Eric	*(Prods Bob's forehead)* Yeah, definitely a Bob. Bit soft in the head. Bob?
Bob	Yes, Eric.
Eric	Am I an Eric?
Bob	*(Nods head slowly)* Yes. A right Eric.
Eric	*(To Blink)* It's official, we're not you.
Blink	Take my word for it, you wouldn't want to be me.
Bob	*(Shrugs shoulders)* So what's the problem, athlete's foot?
Eric	*(Nods towards Blink)* Must be, he's just itching to get on with whatever he wants to be getting on with.
Blink	Story of my life. At my moment of need who should come along but two inept comedians.
Eric	What do you mean, 'inept'? We try our best.
Blink	Just promise me one thing.
Bob	What's that?
Blink	Don't give up your day job.
Eric	Now who's the inept comedian. *(Tuts and turns to Bob)* Listen, *(Cups hand to ear)* I can hear my pillow calling out my name.

Bob	Aw, isn't that sweet.
Eric	We just love spending time together. Come on, let's see if our feet can find their way home.
Blink	If you go now you'll miss out on all the fun.
Eric	Fun? I've had more fun spreading butter with a cocktail stick.
Blink	So you'll understand the way I feel.
Bob	Sorry, I think something got lost in the translation.
Blink	Frustration, the feeling of getting nowhere slowly. The feeling of time laughing as it watches you cultivate wrinkles. The dull ache of consciousness prising your eyelids open in the morning. The sheer exhilaration of watching water disappear down the plug hole. The ...
Eric	*(Interrupts)* Hang on a minute. OK, so life isn't all downhill skiing. So what do you plan to do about it?
Blink	I'm going to jump.
Bob	What's the mask and snorkel for?
Blink	*(Looks at snorkel and hugs it to chest)* Just in case I change my mind when I'm in the water.
	Eric and Bob both look into the water.
Eric	I wouldn't worry about the water.
Blink	*(Peers anxiously into water)* What's wrong with it?
Bob	Oh, there's nothing wrong with the water.
Eric	What bit there is.
Bob	You're more likely to do yourself a mischief on the rusting bike frames and shopping trolleys.
Eric	Not a good choice for your last earthly action.

Blink	Do you mean it might be a bit painful?
Bob	*(Winces and sucks in breath)* Painful? Pain with a capital 'P', mate.
Blink	*(Gets down from the 'bridge' and tucks snorkel under arm)* Blow that for a lark.
Eric	Changed your mind?
Blink	Definitely. I've a good mind to complain to the water authority. Shouldn't let a canal get into such a state. *(Puts arms around Bob and Eric)* Hey, have you heard the one about this bloke with a diving mask and snorkel?
Bob	No, but I think we're about to.

All three walk away, chatting.

'Here I am, in that old place again' by Stuart Garrard and Martin Smith (*The source new songs*, 14).

The feeling of being on your own or rejected seems to happen about as often as you put milk on your cornflakes. In other words, that feeling of being alone in a crowd is part and parcel of life. But does that mean we should just put up with it and concentrate on breathing?

Like many things in life, it's how we react to issues and situations that dictates the way we feel and deal with the trip-wires of life.

Although Jesus knew that death on the cross was essential for the restoring of the relationship between God and his people, this knowledge didn't make the feeling of desolation and rejection any easier to deal with. Jesus was absolutely confident that his father loved him, yet, at that precise moment of agony on the cross, that confidence didn't dull the pain.

In many ways, if we stood back and looked at the issue or situation calmly, we would know that we have people who care for us and want the best for us but, at that exact moment of hurt, it feels as if nothing else counts, nothing can stop us feeling such pain, and the last thing we feel is calm!

We feel like life's loser, everything passes us by and everyone else is OK. The reality, we know, is far different. But it can take a lot of persuasion for us to appreciate that we are not the first person to have ever felt abandoned, rejected or alone. Jesus felt the ultimate rejection and abandonment so that we should never experience total alienation. God is always listening, watching and waiting for us to get to know him better. Even though we may feel alone in a crowded world, we are never out of God's thoughts and only have to avert our eyes from the present situation to experience God's embrace.

1. If Jesus knew that his death on the cross was meant to happen, why did he feel so rejected?

   Christ did not sin or ever tell a lie. Although he was abused, he never tried to get even. And when he suffered, he made no threats. Instead, he had faith in God, who judges fairly. Christ carried the burden of our sins. He was nailed to the cross, so that we would stop sinning and start living right. By his cuts and bruises you are healed. You had wandered away like sheep. Now you have returned to the one who is your shepherd and protector.

   1 Peter 2:22-25

2. Is it wrong to feel rejected or alone?

3. What is the use of being with other people when we feel rejected?

The victim of crucifixion would be made to carry the horizontal beam of his own cross through the streets of the city. After a vicious whipping, the victim was really in no fit shape to carry a heavy, roughly hewn lump of wood around. However the victim made it to the place of crucifixion, it was there that the next stage took place: hammering nails through the hands and the feet fastened to the wooden upright. The pain was intense.

It was the custom of some wealthy women to offer the victims a drink of drugged wine which would deaden the pain. To refuse the drugged wine was to experience the full agony of every nerve-jangling sensation of pain.

'Seasons may change' by Matt Redman (*The source new songs,* 56).

Inner (Have a bag/box of medium-sized stones available. Sit in a dimly lit area.)

Lord,
> this life,
> this journey through
> a landscape
> that's often littered with the debris
> of fear,
> rejection and hurt,
> causes my feet
> to stumble,
> to trip
> and bump
> against every stone
> that attempts
> to batter my spirit,
> causes my eyes to fill
> with the tears of each
> pain-soaked footfall.

(*Take the stones and place them in a pile in front of you*)

Lord,
> each of these stones
> is a reminder,
> a monument to hurt,
> a visible marker
> for others on this journey
> to know that someone else
> has trod the same path.

Lord,
> even though
> in the here and now
> the pain
> seems unbearable,
> it's so good to know

that your Son
trod the path of pain
so that people like me
need never know
the absolute agony
of being separated
from your loving embrace.

Outer

Lord,
    even in the darkness of the night
    and the incessant rainfall
    which threatens to dampen
    the embers of my heart,
    let me always remember
    that your heart
    never grows cold,
    never hardens,
    never turns away
    when those in need
    turn to you
    looking for shelter
    in their dark moments.
Remind me
    that just as you love,
    so should I
    be aware
    of those
    who suffer,
    who hurt,
    who cry out
    from the desolation of their heart.
Wherever my journey takes me,
    wherever my path crosses
    that of another traveller,
    let me be
    as a signpost,
    a guide
    to a well in the desert
    where the tired heart
    can find rest
        shelter
        and drink
        from the water of life.

I thirst

Jesus knew that he had now finished his work. And in order to make the Scriptures come true, he said, 'I am thirsty!' A jar of cheap wine was there. Someone then soaked a sponge with the wine and held it up to Jesus' mouth on the stem of a hyssop plant.　　　John 19:28-29

Soak it up

Two old friends meet in the pub and discuss some of the amazing things that have happened recently. Not least the gossip about a Jew who visited the village's well recently, asked for a drink and then started saying some strange things. He may have been out in the sun too long. The one who thirsts is also the one who offered others the chance to drink from the well that never runs dry.

Characters　Sop and Binge are two of the village 'soaks'. They like nothing better than a lubricant for the throat to enable them to chat about whatever gossip happens to be worth making a bit of a scandal about. If there is no current gossip, they pass the time by inventing potential gossip which the two old soaks will enjoy telling to anyone willing to listen. They are dressed in baggy sweaters, old trousers and worn-out boots.

Scene　The inside of the village watering hole is murky, damp and smelly (and that's just the clientele). The two old soaks sit at a small table with litter covering most of the surface. Each of the old soaks has a large glass of liquid sitting amongst the litter on the table.

Props　Two old sweaters, trousers and boots. A rough-looking table, assorted litter and two large glasses.

You can either depict the interior scene as just the old soaks and the table or complete the scene by adding a few extras and a bar. The sketch starts with the two soaks sipping their drinks against a soundtrack of subdued voices and the occasional snippet of music.

Sop　*(Empties his glass and wipes his mouth across his sleeve)* Ah! I needed that. *(He nods to Binge)* Another one?

Binge   Yeah. Why not? *(Pushes his glass towards Sop)*

Sop   Heard any decent gossip lately?

Binge   I did hear tell that Old Man Armitage found his teeth yesterday. Been missing for three weeks.

Sop   I bet he was glad to get them back.

Binge   He'd been living on soup and grape juice all that time.

Sop   Where'd he find them?

Binge   Over in Zac's field.

Sop   What had he been doing there then? Surely not having a kiss and cuddle with Mrs Armitage? *(Pulls disgusted face)*

Binge   No. He'd been helping Zac spread manure on the field.

Sop   And he lost them . . .

Binge   You've guessed it. Somewhere in the middle of three tonnes of the stuff!

Sop   Hope he washed them well once he got them back.

Binge   Couldn't tell you. His teeth always look a bit stained.

Sop goes to the bar and returns with two full glasses.

Sop   There you go. *(Places glasses on table)* Get your slurping tackle around that.

Binge   *(Licks lips)* Better than a plate of cow's innards this be.

Sop   Oh, I dunno. Nice to have a bit of both, I say. Anyway, enough of this dreaming. Heard any other gossip?

Binge   You'll never guess what happened to me today.

Sop   Let me see. *(Places finger on chin)* How about, you changed your socks in time for the summer?

Binge No. *(Shakes head)* Too early for that. I'll give 'em another month before I change into my summer pair.

Sop Well, *(Frowns)* have you had some success with the cream?

Binge Ooh! You wouldn't believe the agony I go through at night. Not something that I would wish on a camel trader.

Sop Go on, you'll have to tell me.

Binge The wife arrived back from shopping.

Sop Typical. *(Tuts and shakes head)* Nowadays, give 'em a shopping bag and a few coins and they don't stop until the well runs dry.

Binge She said she was only going out to get a loaf.

Sop That's what they all say. The time it takes 'em, you could have ploughed the field, sown the wheat, watched it grow and harvested it in by the time it takes them to fetch a loaf.

Binge You're telling me.

Both take a swig of their drink.

Sop *(Wipes mouth on sleeve)* How long had she been gone, then?

Binge Two years!

Sop Bet the loaf was stale!

Binge She hadn't got a loaf with her.

Sop Bet she got talking and didn't notice the time, eh?

Binge Something like that. Said she came home 'cos she met this weird guy at the well.

Sop He was brave going to the well. That area is a gossip battle zone. It's a wonder he wasn't tongue lashed to death by the female mafia.

Binge *(Shrugs)* Apparently he went at midday when no one else was about.

Sop	Sensible bloke.

Both nod wisely.

Binge	The wife went up to get some water.

Sop	She'd need it to soften the bread.

Binge	The bloke asked her for a drink of water.

Sop	He's definitely not from around here, then.

Binge	He's an out-of-town geezer. Obviously doesn't know the first thing about our customs.

Sop	Yeah. *(Puts down empty glass)* Like how long it takes to get served a beer around here!

Binge	Anyway, he gets talking to the wife, like. And he starts talking daft to her.

Sop	Been out in the sun too long.

Binge	Well, listen to this. He reckons that he can give you 'living water' so that you'll never get thirsty again.

Sop	He don't work for this brewery then, do he!

Binge	You bet he don't. Anyhow, he tells the wife to clear off and come home to me.

Sop	Where else would she be going?

Binge	Well, I ask you. I knew she'd come home eventually. She'd left her purse under the pillow.

Sop	You can always guarantee if they leave their purse under the pillow they'll not be gone long.

Binge	S'right. A woman's heart is where her purse is, I always say.

Sop	Definitely. So what did she say when she came home?

Binge	I'd just got in from feeding the chickens and I heard a voice shout, 'Have you cleaned the goats' pen out?' I knew it was the wife then. Couldn't mistake those honey'd tones of hers.
Sop	You get used to their voices like a pair of well-worn socks.
Binge	Yeah. All comfortable and warm.
Sop	*(Sniffs the air)* Are you sure it's not time to change yours yet?
Binge	*(Sniffs and then looks under table)* Don't think so.
Sop	I think somebody must be burning cabbage, then.
Binge	Disgusting.
Sop	Yeah, absolutely disgusting.

Both pick up their glasses and walk off towards the bar.

'On the cross' by Geoff Baker (*The source new songs,* 48).

To be thirsty is one of the most basic human needs that requires our immediate attention. It's a driving force, something that demands we satisfy that craving for refreshment.

It has always been the custom in many societies to offer anyone a drink when they take a break from their travels or complete their journey. It was also common to provide some water for the traveller to wash their face and sometimes bathe their feet. Even today, when a person visits, one of the first things they are offered is something to drink (we don't seem to go in for the bathing of the feet so much nowadays!).

Jesus was approaching the end of his journey. His trek to the cross had taken him three years of wandering, sharing God's heart, and healing those whose bodies and minds had been in pain. Now, as a final demonstration of God's love, Jesus expressed the desire which echoed the human heart: 'I am thirsty.'

Water is the very element of life. Without it nothing survives. By saying he was 'living water', able to give eternal life, Jesus gave everyone the ability to be reconciled to God.

There is no need for anyone to be thirsty on their journey through life. There is no longer any need for anyone to feel dried-up, parched or suffering as they put one foot in front of the other day by day. Jesus became thirsty, took on the dust of humanity so that our hearts would always have a source of 'living water'. It is no longer 'dust to dust' at the end of our journey but eternal life through God's Son.

1. What was the point of all Jesus' suffering?

   What can we say about all this? If God is on our side, can anyone be against us? God did not keep back his own Son, but he gave him for us. If God did this, won't he freely give us everything else? If God says his chosen ones are acceptable to him, can anyone bring charges against them? Or can anyone condemn them? No indeed! Christ died and was raised to life, and now he is at God's right side, speaking to him for us. Can anything separate us from the love of Christ? Can trouble, suffering, and hard times, or hunger and nakedness, or danger and death? It is exactly as the Scriptures say, 'For you we face death all day long. We are like sheep on their way to be butchered.' In everything we have won more than a victory because of Christ who loves us. I am sure that nothing can separate us from God's love — not life or death, not angels or spirits, not the present or the future, and not powers above or powers below. Nothing in all creation can separate us from God's love for us in Christ Jesus our Lord!

   Romans 8:31-39

2. What, or who, do we turn to when life seems unbearable?

3. Does God's love for us depend on what we do?

When Jesus asked for a drink he was given a sponge soaked in cheap wine (with a distinct tang of vinegar) which was held up to him on the stem of a hyssop plant. The hyssop plant is small and bushy and similar to strong grass, and about 60 centimetres long at best. Therefore, Jesus would have only been head and shoulders above his mother, who would have been able to see every flicker of pain on his face.

'When the cares of life come' by Steve and Vicki Cook (*The source new songs*, 78).

Inner (Place a bowl of water in front of you.)

Lord,
    often
    I grouch,
    I moan,
    I groan,
    complain,
    shout,
    mutter,
    mumble,
    and, occasionally,
    I have been known
    to utter
    a few
    less than choice comments
    about the way I feel.

(Dip hand in water. Lift your hand and allow the drips to fall back into the bowl)

And
    while I'm constantly
    suggesting
    that this isn't the way things should be,
    you're constantly
    reminding me

(Dip hand in water again and lift your hand)

    about how much you love me
    and perhaps
    just occasionally
    it might be preferable
    to hear a few less comments

(Dip hand into the water and then place your hand to your mouth)

    and allow you
    to refresh
    my aching mind,

>   my tired eyes
>   and my dulled senses.
> Lord,
>   creator of life,
>   giver of life,
>   be with me
>   now and for ever.

(Place both hands into the water, lift them and allow the drops to fall back into the bowl).

Outer *(Have a jug of water and several glasses available.)*

> Lord,
>   the voices of the thirsty
>   cry out
>   as we shield our eyes
>   from the biting wind
>   and stinging dust
>   that attempt to stifle our cries.

(Give everyone a glass of water)

> Lord,
>   your love
>   refreshes,
>   reassures
>   that we are never alone,
>   never without a hope,
>   never without someone
>   to walk each step of the way.

(Take a sip of water)

> Lord,
>   take our lives
>   and encourage us
>   to be as one voice,
>   calling in the desert
>   to those who thirst
>   to come to the one
>   who provides
>   streams in the barren land,
>   which bring life
>   where death once prevailed.
> Lord,
>   let your love flow
>   to and through each one of us.

It is finished

After Jesus drank the wine, he said, 'Everything is done!' He bowed his head and died. John 19:30

The ragged trade

They think it's all over . . . well . . . it's only just begun. How easy it is to think that death means the end, the finish, the completion of all that went before. How wrong can you get?

Characters Bill and Ben are two market stall traders. Neither of them likes to miss an opportunity to ply their trade whatever the circumstances. Both are dressed in denim jackets, cloth caps and bright T-shirts.

Scene It's the end of a busy trading day. Bill and Ben still have a few items for sale and are not too willing to leave while there still might be the possibility of a sale. Both are standing behind a stall on which a few items remain. The weather has taken a turn for the worse and both Bill and Ben are feeling the chill.

Props Denim jackets, brightly coloured T-shirts, two tables with a selection of items scattered on them. Recording of crowd noises and the occasional crack of thunder.

Bill *(Pulls collar of jacket up and shivers)* So that's it then. It's finished.

Ben Looks like it. *(Looks up at sky)*

Bill It's a pity.

Ben Yeah. Shame really.

Bill *(Nods)* A real waste.

Ben A crying shame.

Bill	An opportunity wasted.	
Ben	Well, not that wasted, surely.	
Bill	No, not totally.	
Ben	It's not been all bad.	
Bill	*(Shrugs)* No, that's true.	
Ben	There were some good moments.	
Bill	One or two. *(Frowns)* Could have been better, though.	
Ben	Yeah. Just a bit.	
Bill	Still, can't complain, can we.	
Ben	We shouldn't really.	
Bill	We've had a good run, haven't we.	
Ben	Not too bad.	
Bill	It's a pity, though.	
Ben	*(Nods in agreement)* Yeah. Real pity.	
Bill	Oh well, there's always another day.	
Ben	*(Looks at Bill enquiringly)* Hey, we're not done yet, are we?	
Bill	What do you mean?	
Ben	We've still got all this stock left. *(Points to several items on the table)*	
Bill	*(Shrugs and holds hands out)* The punters are all going home now.	
Ben	Wait a minute. *(Looks around anxiously)* Isn't there anyone else to crucify?	
Bill	Doubt it. It's getting a bit late. Anyway, *(Looks skywards)* it's gone all dark. Bet there's rain on the way. *(Pulls cap down over eyes)*	

Ben	Don't give up so easily. Look, *(Points towards audience)* offer that bloke over there a free sample if he'll go and get himself arrested and crucified.
Bill	*(Lifts cap up)* Free sample won't do him much good then, will it!
Ben	It's all business. Never turn down an opportunity.
Bill	That's what I admire about you.
Ben	What's that, then?
Bill	Your willingness to offer someone a deal that's always worth refusing.
Ben	*(Sniffs)* Never been known to miss a potential customer.
Bill	*(Nods knowingly)* Don't they know it!
Ben	*(Taps chest)* You can always rely on me. And that's more than can be said for some of these blokes *(Points into distance)* who go and get themselves crucified.
Bill	*(Sighs)* You're all heart.
Ben	Well, you can't go letting folk down by going and getting yourself put out of business. Don't make sense. *(Rearranges some of the items on the table)*
Bill	Perhaps it wasn't their fault. They might have been set up. You never know.
Ben	What are you talking about. Are you suggesting a conspiracy theory.
Bill	I've heard stranger things.
Ben	You've been indulging in the fermented camel's milk again, haven't you.
Bill	No, seriously, I've heard rumours that the local big noises don't like anybody making trouble on their patch. *(Looks around anxiously)*
Ben	That's OK. I don't stand for any nonsense on my patch either.
Bill	Yeah, but you don't go and crucify them, do you? *(Rearranges some of the items on the table)*

Ben	I make them feel damned uncomfortable if that's what you mean. *(Picks up an item, looks at it for a few seconds and then bangs it down onto the table)*
Bill	Hey! Don't do that. Made me jump, you did. Anyway, I mean, you wouldn't go to such extremes as to have them permanently silenced, would you?
Ben	From what I hear, that was one of the problems with a bloke that was hung up today. *(Sniffs and buttons jacket up)*
Bill	What's that?
Ben	Couldn't gag him. So they had to employ other, less subtle methods. *(Taps side of nose)* Know what I mean?
Bill	*(Snort of indignation)* Don't call crucifixion subtle.
Ben	Works though, don't it?
Bill	From what I hear, that bloke said it was only a temporary measure.
Ben	Leave it out. You can't very well be hung up with nails and then after a few minutes shout, 'OK, I'm sorry. I've had enough, you can let me down now.' The authorities would be a laughing stock.
Bill	No. What I mean is, that bloke said they couldn't kill him.
Ben	They had a damn good try.
Bill	He said he would die and then come back to life.
Ben	Best bit of marketing I've ever heard. Perhaps we should try that. *(Turns to audience and shouts)* 'Hey, come and get your sandals here. *(Waves an imaginary pair of sandals)* They'll never wear out, they've got an eternal sole!'
Bill	You're just a hard-headed, ignorant opportunist.
Ben	That's the nicest thing anyone's ever said about me.

Both begin to tidy the items on the table as the lights go down.

'All my days' by Stuart Townend (*The source new songs*, 2).

The dark clouds, the thunder and chill in the air must have been enough to convince most of the onlookers that it really *was* finished. It was the end of all they had hoped and dreamed of. The crucifixion had put an end to every promise and vague expectation . . . or had it?

The mood that afternoon was one of extreme sadness and disappointment. Jesus had been mocked: 'He can save others but he can't save himself' and a board put above his head declaring: 'King of the Jews'. Not only were the taunts and barbed comments aimed at Jesus, they were directed at anyone who believed that Jesus was God's Son, the Saviour. To underline the point, Jesus was seen by everyone to be humiliated, whipped and nailed up on a cross just the same as anyone who dared to challenge the civil and religious authorities. And now, from his own lips, Jesus admits, 'It is finished'.

You can imagine the number of heads that were lowered in despair and sadness. But it was only a matter of days since Jesus had reminded his disciples again of what lay ahead:

> *Jesus left with his disciples and started through Galilee. He did not want anyone to know about it, because he was teaching the disciples that the Son of Man would be handed over to people who would kill him. But three days later he would rise to life. The disciples did not understand what Jesus meant, and they were afraid to ask.*   Mark 9:30-32

Even if they had remembered, would they have taken the comment about rising after three days as just another false hope?

For Jesus, the words 'It is finished' were a statement that he had accomplished what he set out to do. The journey from virgin birth to crucifixion had been completed. It was never meant to be a statement of 'So, that's that, then. It was nice while it lasted!' It was the sole purpose of Jesus' ministry to reconcile humanity with God. The relationship no longer depended on animal sacrifice and the priestly rituals. From that point on anyone could approach God and develop a relationship with the creator. For Jesus, not so much a full stop at the end of a life but a question mark. A sort of 'now it's up to you. What are you going to do about your relationship with God?'

1. What does Jesus' death mean to me?

   Now we see how God does make us acceptable to him. The Law and the Prophets tell how we become acceptable, and it isn't by obeying the Law of Moses. God treats everyone alike. He accepts people only because they have faith in Jesus Christ. All of us have sinned and fallen short of God's glory. But God treats us much better than we deserve, and because of Christ Jesus, he freely accepts us and sets us free from our sins. God sent Christ to be our sacrifice. Christ offered his life's blood, so that by faith in him we could come to God. And God did this to show that in the past he was right to be patient and forgive sinners. This also shows that God is right when he accepts people who have faith in Jesus. Romans 3:21-26

2. How does God forgive us?

3. Does knowing that God has forgiven us make it any easier for us to forgive other people?

The word: 'bowed' in John 19:30, literally means to deliberately put the head back into a position of rest. Far from Jesus throwing back his head in a cry of pain and anguish, he placed his head as if he were settling back after the completion of a hard task, a sigh of achievement, of finishing what he set out to do. Which, after all, is what he had done!

'There's a new song arising' by Darrell Evans (*The source new songs*, 66).

Inner (Sit on a chair in the centre of the room to give the feeling of isolation.)

Lord,
    I'm really finding life
    kind of frustrating.
So many things
    demanding my attention,
    wanting my time,
    eating away at my sanity
    until
    I can't remember
    what it was I was supposed to be doing
    in the first place.
Sometimes
    I walk into a room
    and then spend the next ten minutes
    wondering what I'm doing there!
I look around me for a sign,
    a clue to my action.
        Why, when, how, what for?
And, Lord,
    if I'm honest
    that's exactly how I feel
    when I go to church.
It's not that I don't want to be there
    but it would be nice
    if I had a clue
    as to what I was supposed to be doing there!
It's a good job that my faith
    isn't in tradition, buildings or committees,
    or even in how many times
    someone remembers my name,
    but my faith is in the one
    who gave his all for me.

Outer (Stand up with the chair remaining behind you. Begin the prayer by facing north.)

Lord,
    let us never forget
    all those people
    who feel that they've come to the end.
Their strength has left them
    and it's just too much trouble
    to put one foot in front of the other.
(Turn to the west)
And, Lord,
    let us not forget
    all those people
    who feel the pressure
    of living up to other people's expectations,
    where the quality of your life
    is measured by the accumulation
    of material wealth.
(Turn to the south)
Lord,
    let us not forget
    all those people
    who feel the oppression
    of regimes
    that fear the expression
    of a human heart.
(Turn to the east)
And Lord,
    let us not forget
    all those people
    who suffer hatred,
    violence,
    and are forced to live
    as foreigners
    in their own land.
Lord,
    let us not forget.

Father, I give you my life

Around midday the sky turned dark and stayed that way until the middle of the afternoon. The sun stopped shining, and the curtain in the temple split down the middle. Jesus shouted, 'Father, I put myself in your hands!' then he died. When the Roman officer saw what had happened, he praised God and said, 'Jesus must really have been a good man!'

Luke 23:44-49

A legal wrangle?

Who is to blame for this charade, this miscarriage of justice? Is anyone willing to take the blame and admit that they may have got it wrong? Two judges discuss the events of the day and consider their part in the proceedings. A question of guilt and legal justice are discussed along with the possibility that they may, sometimes, get it wrong. But still, they haven't had any complaints yet . . . TOUCH WOOD.

Characters Ale and Wine are two representatives of the ever-popular legal profession. They've just finished another gruelling day administering justice according to the time-honoured code of class and wealth. Wine is confident in his ability to perform as expected while Ale isn't too sure that everything they do is quite as it should be.

Scene The changing-room of the justice department. Ale and Wine are preparing to get out of their legal robes and put on their casual wear. The noise of the courtroom and gallery can still be heard in the background.

Props Black robes and white, curly wigs and shoes. Two benches with lockers or hat and coat stand.

Ale and Wine should enter together murmuring about the day's proceedings. They flop down on the benches, tired and hungry. In the background the noise of a crowd can be heard along with the occasional shout of 'injustice' and the slamming of a cell door. As the two sit down the sound of a cell door slamming shut reverberates around the room.

Ale	*(Sighs)* I'm glad that's all finished with.	
Wine	Thank goodness. *(Kicks shoes across the floor)*	
Ale	I wouldn't want to go through that again in a hurry.	
Wine	Come on, it's all part of the job. *(Massages feet)*	
Ale	What are you doing that for? *(Points to Wine's feet)*	
Wine	What?	
Ale	Moulding your toe jam into abstract shapes.	
Wine	*(Stops massaging feet and wipes hands on robes)* Makes me feel better.	
Ale	Better for what? It's not as if you're standing up all day.	
Wine	I know, I know, I sit down all day, but rubbing my feet helps the circulation and, hopefully, the blood will flow upwards from there. Anyway, you do what you have to do.	
Ale	But do you have to rub your feet so vigorously? All it seems to do is redistribute the odour.	
Wine	*(Sniffs)* I can't smell anything.	
Ale	What's normal to some is something less than pleasant for others.	
Wine	Bit like our job really. Sentencing criminals to a wood and nail diet is normal for us but not too pleasant for them.	
Ale	I know, but it's never easy.	
Wine	Look, they know the score. If they can't take the punishment, don't do the crime.	
Ale	I still don't like it.	
Wine	Listen, *(Wags finger at Ale)* we're paid to make decisions.	
Ale	But how do we know we've made the right decisions?	
Wine	The evidence!	

Ale	But that's not always clear cut, is it?
Wine	Maybe not. But we know they're criminals, they know they're criminals, so what if the evidence doesn't match up?
Ale	But it's all circumstantial.
Wine	*(Shakes head slowly from side to side)* Any evidence is *good* evidence.
Ale	OK. Supposing we say we've got a witness, he was blind drunk at the time and wouldn't recognise a choir of angels at a barn dance, but is willing to testify (for a barrel of grape gut rot) that he definitely saw the accused on the night in question acting in a suspicious manner.
Wine	*(Folds arms across chest)* Nothing wrong with that.
Ale	*(Leans forward)* But it's false evidence.
Wine	So what do you propose? Let them all go with a caution, pat them on the head and tell them to behave? *(Holds hands in front, palms upwards)*
Ale	At least they've another chance.
Wine	Another chance to commit a crime again. You have to nip crime in the bud.
Ale	What do you suggest, throw babies into prison on suspicion that in twenty years' time they may, if we can find a blind, deaf and dumb witness, be involved in something vaguely illegal?
Wine	*(Sighs and shakes head from side to side)* You really haven't got a stomach for this type of work, have you?
Ale	I thought a judge was supposed to uphold the law.
Wine	We do. *(Nods head)*
Ale	How can you say that when we've just sentenced an innocent man *(Waves arm in general direction of stage left)* to be crucified for nothing more than getting on the authorities' nerves?
Wine	*(Pause)* They're never innocent.
Ale	The authorities? No one is innocent when they're up before you.

Wine	You know I never prejudge a case, ho, ho. But seriously, if I listened to the whole debate and cross-examined every donkey in town it would take forever, and then *(Points finger at Ale)* who would be in trouble with the authorities?
Ale	But we're here to help the democratic process.
Wine	Look, I choose to be here, the authorities choose to pay me – that's democracy.
Ale	A bit limited in its application?
Wine	That's the way it works. If you gave every Matthew, Mary and Martha the chance to abuse the democratic process we'd have queues forming all the way to Rome. You have to draw the line somewhere.
Ale	And where's your line?
Wine	At the bottom of my bank balance, next to the word 'total', followed by a very large numerical figure. If they've got the money (and we all know money talks, especially when it calls my name), then they are part of the local elite, and that's good enough for me.
Ale	So if someone is part of the local sailing club or a member of the gravel pit pitch and putt, or even part of the sauna and scrub set, then they're OK in your books.
Wine	As long as their name is in my accounts ledger then they're all right by me. Anyway, it's all a matter of who you know and who you don't.
Ale	So, if you can afford it your face fits; if you can't you're a nobody?
Wine	Nothing wrong with that. Nobody misses a nobody, do they?
Ale	Except for the other nobodies.
Wine	*(Makes fist with one hand and smacks it into the other open palm)* But they don't count. I've already made that point.
Ale	Well, we just have to think ourselves lucky we're in such a fortunate position.
Wine	Precisely. We run an efficient court here. Never had any complaints, touch wood. *(Looks around for some wood to touch and then settles for tapping Ale's head)*

Ale	*(Rubs head)* Mind the splinters. *(Wipes forehead)* I just think it's a bit difficult when those who want to make a complaint are nailed up. Just a tad awkward to write a note to your local politician isn't it.
Wine	That's why we don't have any complaints.
Ale	I suppose you're right. Once they're stitched up, banged up, and then nailed up, getting the evidence together for an appeal is slightly difficult.
Wine	Of course it is. That's why it pays *(Nudges Ale on the shoulder)* to decide the sentence before you see the criminal's eyes. Can't have none of this belly-aching 'I'm innocent, your honour' business. Listen to that and before you know it you're hearing all about their poor old grandmother and the trouble she has with her hip.
Ale	I must have heard that one a dozen times. The only 'hip' trouble the granny has is making sure her hip flask is full. *(Frowns)* I just don't like the thought that we could have made a mistake, that's all.
Wine	Don't worry yourself about it. It'll all blow over.
Ale	I hope so. I couldn't live with myself if I found out I'd made a mistake.
Wine	Let's face it. The dead couldn't live with it either!
Ale	It's a good job they can't. Make a hell of a mess filling out the complaint form. Can you imagine 'place of residence, sir?'
Wine	No fixed abode!
Ale	No address, no redress, eh?
Wine	Exactly. Now stop worrying and let's get down to the canteen and have ourselves a spot of lunch.
Ale	Good idea. All that sentencing works up an appetite.
Wine	It surely does. Come on before we miss out on that fig crumble.
Ale	Never missed it yet. Touch wood.

Ale and Wine take off their robes and walk off stage.

'Our Father who art in heaven' by Paul Field and Stephen Deal (*The source new songs*, 51).

Doing the right thing: something we would prefer to do (well, most of the time) but find it difficult to know *how* to do it and *if* we've achieved it.

Sometimes knowing that we've done the right thing is relatively simple. The box of chocolates, bunch of flowers, birthday present or jar of pickled gherkins usually gets a quick response with a thank-you or huge smile from the recipient (or a sickly grin in the case of the pickled gherkins). Knowing whether we should enrol on a particular course of study or accept an offer of a job are not quite so easy.

In Jesus' case, knowing what to do wasn't the problem. Even knowing how things would turn out wasn't difficult to come to terms with. Convincing other people that he was doing the right thing *was* the problem.

Jesus accepted the crucifixion not from an acknowledgement of guilt but because he knew that's what his Father wanted him to do. However, even knowing the path to tread didn't make life, or death, any easier.

Throughout his life Jesus had decisions to make. Some decisions were easy, an automatic response to someone's need. Other decisions required thought and a lot of chatting to his Father. Although Jesus knew how to do the right thing, and why, he had to trust that God the Father had everything under control.

You can read the Gospels and think that Jesus was always going to do the right thing because God had told him what to do, how to do it and what would happen when he did. But even that didn't make the situation easy. Jesus cried, sweated and bled about the course of action that God had asked him to take. Jesus agonised over the details and whether there wasn't another way of doing what God wanted. In the end doing the right thing was all that mattered.

Our life choices may never be so demanding of us. But the decisions we make affect so many areas of our lives, and the lives of others, that doing the right thing is just as important.

Jesus had to place his trust in God. He had to have faith in God's actions. Even more importantly, he continually chatted with his father about whatever situation he faced.

The same applies to us. We need to place our trust in God and have faith that he is looking after us every step of the way. And, just as Jesus did, we too need to constantly chat with God, even if it's to say: 'This is tougher than I expected!' or 'Haven't you got any better ideas?' Doing the right thing starts with God and ends with God. If we involve God at the beginning, then even though we may stumble and fall over at times, we'll have someone with us who will laugh with us, cry with us and encourage us to keep going when the going gets tough. Whatever the outcome, doing the right thing means getting God involved.

1. So, what does doing the right thing mean?

   Don't worry about anything, but pray about everything. With thankful hearts offer up your prayers and requests to God. Then, because you belong to Christ Jesus, God will bless you with peace that no one can completely understand. And this peace will control the way you think and feel. Finally, my friends, keep your minds on whatever is true, pure, right, holy, friendly, and proper. Don't ever stop thinking about what is truly worthwhile and worthy of praise. Philippians 4:6-8

2. Does prayer really have any effect?

3. What should we do when things go wrong?

As Jesus died the curtain in the temple split down the middle. The curtain screened the Most Holy Place, where the blood of the sacrifice was poured on the altar once a year, out of the view of everyone except the High Priest. The curtain was a symbol of the power of the High Priest; only he had the authority to go beyond the curtain which separated God and the people.

When Jesus died the curtain ripped from top to bottom. Not only did the torn curtain indicate that the power of the priests had come to an end, but also that God had made the tear, from the top and not by the people. The sacrifice of Jesus, on the altar of the cross, dealt with sin for all time.

'We come into your presence with singing' by Russell Fragar and Darlene Zschech (*The source new songs*, 74).

Inner (Light a candle and place it directly in front of you.)

Lord,
    well, it's kind of difficult.
I suppose that with all your omniscience
    you know what's going on
    or what's supposed to be happening
    but isn't turning out
    according to plan.
I thought everything was fine
    until everything fell apart
    like the proverbial pack of cards.
And now
    here I am,
    wanting to know
    what on earth you were doing
    which took your mind off my situation?
Am I so inconsequential?
Or were things wrong
    from the beginning?
I really did think
    that I knew what I was doing
    even though
    I hadn't got a clue
    what was going on, down and along
    until I started
    to go under.
So, here I am.
Better late than never
    I always say.
I would have chatted sooner
    but I was so busy
    doing this, that and the other,
    and thought
    you might be a touch busy
    dealing with all those things
    that occupy
    the creator of all things.
And now,
    having realised
    that I've put my foot in it
    big time,
    I thought

    I'd better get around
    to asking
    how we're going
    to sort this mess out?
I know it might seem a cheek
    to ask for your help
    after the event,
    but, as I said earlier,
    better late than never.
I can't promise
    I'll do things any different
    the next time,
    but it's good to know
    that you're a very forgiving sort,
    which is just as well
    because,
    although I don't mean to,
    I somehow always forget
    to check things out with you first,
    but still,
    I get around to it,
    eventually.
And, as I always say,
    better late than never.

Outer (Ask every person in the room to light a candle and place it in front of them.)

Lord,
    all over the world
    there must be people
    asking, crying, shouting out
    for your help
    in situations
    that make our problems
    seem insignificant.
But I know that you care
    and watch out
    for each and every single one of us
    no matter
    who we are
    or what we've done.

TOUCH WOOD

> I can't pretend to understand
> > or begin to comprehend
> > why some things happen
> > which make us question,
> > or even stare in disbelief.
> But nothing happens
> > without your knowing
> > every single detail,
> > of every situation
> > of every person
> > everywhere,
> > all over the world.
> And even though
> > my head can't take it all in
> > I thank you again
> > for loving each and every one of us
> > unconditionally.
> Hours, days,
> > and even months may pass
> > without you hearing a word
> > from our lips,
> > and still you care
> > about every situation,
> > every person,
> > everywhere,
> > all over the world.

ISBN 1 84003 266 9
Catalogue No. 1500230

Intended to annoy, disturb, raise a smile, and generally get under your skin, *Parallels* uses contemporary versions of the Bible passages for Lent to explore issues which affect us daily.

Pete encourages us to read and study but also to argue – with each other and God – as he unpacks themes which make us question, think and even act.

ISBN 1 84003 543 9
Catalogue No. 1500351

Welcome to the world of De'ath, the merciless chat show host. Join with him as he probes the minds of the guests, snore with him as he falls asleep in front of the audience and squirm as you realise that you know some of the guests a little too well . . .

Each sketch requires only two people and is suitable for use in churches, youth groups and schools. Use the sketches individually to fit in with a theme you are looking at, or put several together and perform a show. At the end of each sketch is a question to encourage discussion, followed by a Bible passage which looks at the topic from God's point of view.

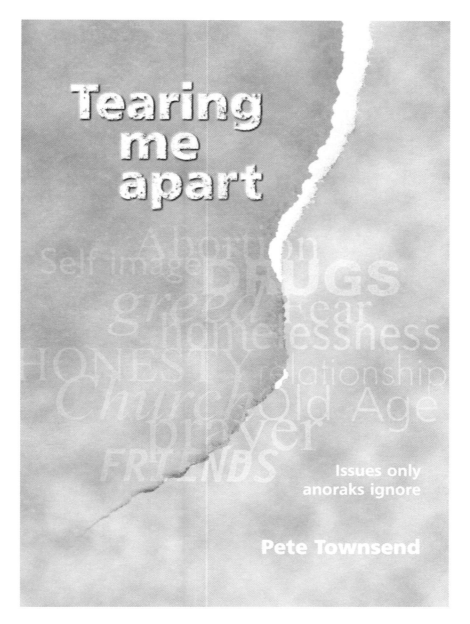

ISBN 1 84003 456 4
Catalogue No. 1500320

Abortion, drugs, relationships, Church, homelessness – there are so many issues and situations in life which can make us feel out of our depth. *Tearing me apart* looks at some of these and the impact they have on us and the people we come into contact with. As you read the book and confront the various subjects raised, you will be challenged to chat with God as you explore what he has to say about things.